Decodable Readers 33–41

LTX
1-004
Sco
dec
33-41

Scott Foresman

Editorial Offices: Glenview, Illinois • New York, New York
Sales Offices: Reading, Massachusetts • Duluth, Georgia
Glenview, Illinois • Carrollton, Texas • Menlo Park, California

Printed in the United States of America

ISBN 0-673-65180-0

2 3 4 5 6 7 8 9 10 - BISF - 06 05 04 03 02 01 00

Contents

Dean's Neat Green Cast

by Dona R. McDuff
illustrated by Clive Scruton

Dean and Sid like to
ride sleds.

Dean and Sid can race on
sleds. Dean likes to beat Sid.

One time Dean and Sid
went fast.

Dean fell. His sled tipped.
Dean broke his leg. He needed
help.

Dean's dad called Jean.
Dean went to see Jean. She
checked his leg.

"You broke your leg. You broke this bone. We will help it heal."

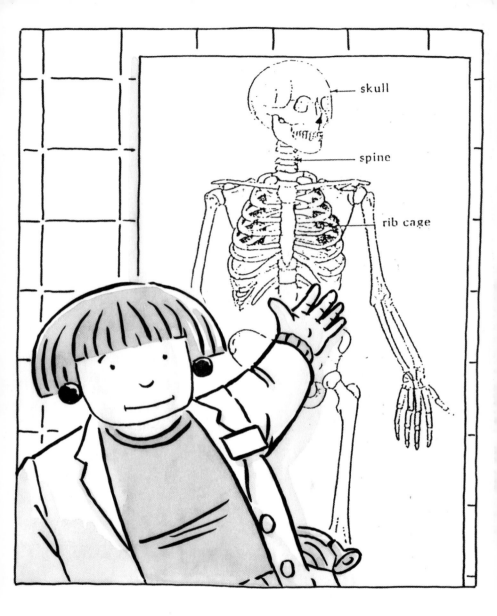

"We have 206 bones."

"Bones can't bend," she said.
"Bones help you run and jump.
Bones are like a frame."

Jean asked Dean to pick his
cast. Did Dean pick a red cast
or a green cast?

Dean picked green.

"Green is neat," Dean said.

"Bones need to heal. This
cast will help. Keep it clean.
We will check it in six weeks."

"Six weeks!" Dean yelled.
"That's a long time!"

Dean seemed sad.

"We'll get a treat," said Dad.

"We will stop for ice cream."

Dean sat at the shop. Sid sat
next to him.

"That's a neat cast!" Sid said.

"Sled ride?" Sid asked

"I will call you!" Dean grinned.

Phonics Skill Long *e* spelled *ea:* *Dean, beat, Jean, heal, neat, clean, treat, cream*

Phonics Skill Inflected Ending -*ed* (with and without spelling change: doubling final consonants): *tipped, needed, called, checked, asked, picked, yelled, seemed, grinned*

Spelling Words: *clean, asked, called*

Ray's Fire Bell

by Sydnie Meltzer Kleinhenz
illustrated by George Ulrich

Ray is our pet.

He will not stay in his tank.

He may walk all over this class.

We like painting.

Vail makes a mess.

He gets paint on his hands.

He will clean himself up inside.

Vail hears the fire bell!
He will not wait.
Vail runs outside.

Mr. Bails runs out.

"No fire," he tells Miss Fay.

"Who rang that bell?" asks
Miss Fay.

"Who rang that bell?" we kids all ask.

"I didn't see who rang it," he tells us.

We all go back inside.

Vail, May, and Clay sit at desks.

Ray sits on Vail's desk.

He's glad to sit in the sun.

The next day we play outside.
Jay needs a pail. It's for sand.
Miss Fay lets Jay get it.
Jay hears the fire bell! Jay runs.

Mr. Bails runs outside.

"No fire," he tells us.

"Who rang that bell?" asks Jay.

"Who rang that bell?" we all
ask him.

"I didn't see who rang it," he
tells us.

We like feeding the birds.

We need seeds. Faith gets them
from Miss Fay's desk.

Faith hears the fire bell!

"Wait!" yells Faith. She sees Ray.
"Ray went up when we went out.
He made the fire bell ring!"

Phonics Skill Long *a* Spelled *ai, ay:* *Ray, stay, may, painting, Vail, paint, wait, Bails, Fay, May, Clay, day, play, Jay, pail, Faith*

Phonics Skill Contractions: *didn't, he's, it's*

Spelling Words: *play, may, wait*

Let's Play!

REVIEW

by Stefanie Langer
illustrated by Marcy Ramsey

"Can we play?" asked
Beth.

"Wait, and I will ask my
mom," said Kay.

"May I play with Beth?"
asked Kay.

"Yes," said Mom, "but
we will eat at six. Be cleaned
up then."

"Can Beth stay and eat
with us?" asked Kay.

"Yes, she can stay," said
Mom. "I will call Beth's
mom."

"What can we play?"
asked Beth.

"It may rain," said Kay.
"Let's stay inside. We can
play games."

"It's a deal," said Beth.

"Can we play tag?" asked
Beth.

"Not inside!" called Kay.
"My mom will not like that!"

"Can we jump rope?"
asked Beth.

"Not inside!" said Kay.
"My mom will not like that!"

"Can we play class?"
asked Beth.

"We can play class
inside," said Kay. "I like to
play that!"

"I will teach," said Kay. "I will teach math now."

"Not math!" yelled Beth. "May I paint or play with clay?"

"No," said Kay. "It's math test time. Sit at this desk."

"This is not fun. Can we please eat treats?" asked Beth.

"Yes, we can eat treats," said Kay, "but we must clean up."

"I can eat treats and take a math test," called Beth.

"Look!" called Kay. "The
rain has stopped. It's a nice
day."

"Let's play!" said Beth.

Phonics Skill Long *e* Spelled *ea*: *eat, cleaned, deal, teach, please, treats, clean*

Phonics Skill Inflected Ending *–ed*: *asked, cleaned, yelled, called, stopped*

Phonics Skill Long *a* spelled *ai, ay*: *play, wait, Kay, may, stay, rain, paint, clay, day*

Phonics Skill Contractions: *let's, it's*

Spelling Words: *ask, asked, call, called, clean, cleaned, play, may, wait, rain*

Duck's Coat

by Judy Nayer
illustrated by Laura Rader

Duck had a coat.

It didn't fit.

The coat will not grow.

Duck needed a coat that fit.

Duck went shopping.
She shopped at a big sale.
At last she saw a coat.
It fit. Duck got it.

Duck went home.

She showed Hen her old coat.

Duck did not need it.

Duck gave Hen the coat.

Duck went home. She sat to read.
Then Duck jumped up.

"I can show my new coat," said
Duck.

Duck didn't see her coat.
"Help!" Duck moaned. "My coat
is missing!"

"My coat is lost. Did you see
it?" Duck asked.

She asked Goat.

He was floating in his rowboat.

She asked Crow on her way to
see a show.

She asked Toad.

He was fixing the road.

She asked Sheep.

Sheep was towing her jeep.

She asked Skunk.
She was loading a big trunk.
She asked Mole.
He was digging a huge hole.

At last she asked Fox.

He was getting on his socks.

"Did you check in the coat box?" Fox asked.

Duck ran home.

She didn't stop.

Duck needed that coat.

It was sitting in its box!

Phonics Skill Long *o* Spelled *oa, ow:* *coat, grow, showed, show, moaned, Goat, floating, rowboat, Crow, Toad, road, towing, loading*

Phonics Skill Inflected Ending *-ing* (with and without spelling change: doubling final consonants): *shopping, missing, floating, fixing, towing, loading, digging, getting, sitting*

Spelling Words: *grow, show, floating*

It's Just Right!

by John Everett
illustrated by Jackie Urbanovic

Jill is Pam's pal.

Jill and Pam have fun.

Jill's cat plays with its tail.

The cat's tail is long.
Jill's cat can chase its tail.
Pam likes Jill's cat. She
likes it a lot.

Jill's cat is so nice. It is small and sweet.

It is just right for Jill.

Pam sighs. She wants
a cat like Jill's.

"I'll play with it each
night," Pam says.

Mom and Dad and Pam
eat lunch. Pam has pie.
Then Dad hands Pam a gift.

"Can it be a cat?" Pam asks.
"Peek inside and see," Dad
tells Pam.

It is Pam's stuffed cat.

"This is my old cat," Pam
tells them.

"It has a note tied on its neck.
Read it," Dad tells Pam.

Pam must go to a bright
light. She reads Dad's note.

Pam sighs.

Pam's mom smiles.

"Let's look," she tells Pam.

Pam looks left. She does not
see anything.

"Look right," Dad tells Pam.

Pam sees a black thing.

The black thing is a cat.
She picks up Dad's gift. She
holds it tight.

It feels just right!

Phonics Skill Long *i* Spelled *igh, ie:* *right, sighs, night, pie, tied, bright, light, tight*

Phonics Skill Possessives (singular): *Pam's, cat's, Jill's, Dad's*

Spelling Words: *pie, tie(d), light, right*

Night Sights

REVIEW

by Paulinda Russell
illustrated by Cheryl Kirk Noll

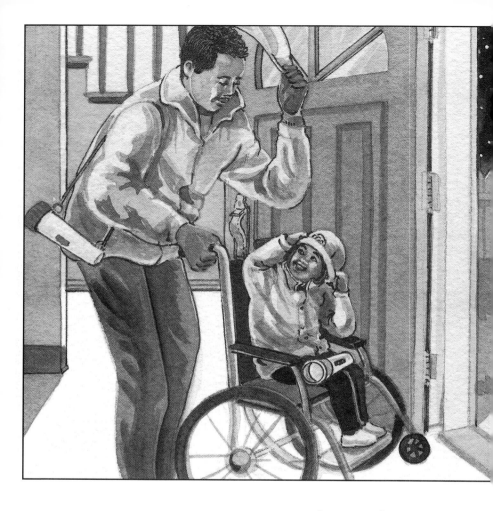

Let's go on a night ride!
We'll need coats and
flashlights. We'll need mittens
and hats.

See and feel the night.
Feel that night chill! See the
night's sights. See who likes
nighttime.

See that pond. Frogs and
toads play at night. See them
hopping and jumping and
croaking. Fish swim in that
pond. Can fish sleep?

It's late at night, but ducks
still float on the pond. Can
ducks sleep and float at the
same time?

Plants need sunlight. Can
plants grow at night?

See that plant's shadow?
It is big! See that tree's
shadow? Is it growing? It's
a sight!

See that path? See that
mask? Can she see us? She
sleeps in the daytime, and
she eats at night. She feels
right eating late at night.

See that street? Streetlights make shadows.

Cats sit on trash cans. Cats screech and fight at night.

See the lights in those homes? Dogs lie in lighted windows inside. Can those dogs see us at night? Will those dogs wake up?

Let's go home. It's time to
end this night ride. We'll get
milk and pie. We'll dream
about the night's sights.

Phonics Skill Long *o* Spelled *oa, ow:* *coats, toads, croaking, float, grow, shadow, shadows, growing, windows*

Phonics Skill Inflected Ending *-ing:* *hopping, jumping, croaking, growing, eating*

Phonics Skill Long *i* Spelled *igh, ie:* *night, flashlights, night's, sights, nighttime, sunlight, sight, right, streetlights, fight, lights, lie, lighted, pie*

Phonics Skill Singular Possessives: *night's, plant's, tree's*

Spelling Words: *grow, float, show, growing, lie, pie, night, light, right*

My Mail

by Heather Devonshire
illustrated by George Ulrich

My name is Molly. I like
getting mail. Each day I check
my mailbox. Many times I don't
get mail. It is still fun to check.

I like sending notes in the
mail. Each note needs a stamp.
It's fun licking and sticking on
cute stamps. Mail can't be sent
without stamps.

I am sending notes to Kathy
and Ty. Kathy's home is close
by, but Ty lives in Seaside City.

I take my notes to the
mailbox. It is right on my block.
My mom walks with me. I drop
my mail in the slot.

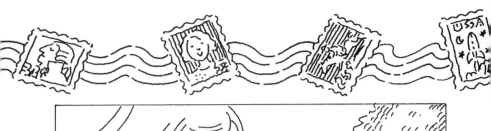

We read the note on the
mailbox. Pickup is at three.
We will wait to see where my
notes will go next!

We tell funny jokes as we
wait. Then a mail truck stops
right by us.

Jane gets out of the truck. She checks the mailbox. Then she takes out a bin filled with mail.

Jane places the bin in the truck.
We wait as she places this bin
back inside the mailbox.

I tell Jane that she has my notes
in her mail truck. I peek in Jane's
mail truck. It is stuffed with mail.

Jane tells me all about mail.

"When will Kathy and Ty get my notes?" I ask.

"This mail will fly!" Jane tells me.

We wave as Jane leaves.

Jane was right. It didn't take long. Kathy and Ty got my notes. I am glad!

Phonics Skills Vowel Sounds of *y*: *my, Molly, many, Kathy, Ty, City, funny, by, fly*

Phonics Skill Compound Words: *mailbox, without, Seaside, pickup, inside*

Spelling Words: *funny, many, my, fly*

What's New with Sue?

by Myka-Lynne Sokoloff
illustrated by Andy Levine

This is Sue.
What is new with Sue?
Sue can chew gum.
She is big!

This is little Sue.
She makes wishes.
What does she wish?
This is a clue: Gum

Sue gets a few boxes.
Then she sees herself chew.
She chews and blows.
She can't do it!

Sue sees Drew blow.
Drew teaches Sue.

Sue chews and chews.
Then Sue blows.
She blows till she is blue!
Sue will not give up.

One day, Sue blew and blew.
The gum grew and grew!
It is true!

Can Drew save Sue?
He wishes he had a way.

Pop!
The gum flew on Sue!
It sticks like glue!
What can Sue do?
This is a clue:

Sue is sad and blue.
What can Mom do?

Mom kisses Sue.
Then she helps.
Sue gets a trim.

Look at Sue!
That cut is new.
She can blow and chew!

Phonics Skill Vowel Patterns *ew, ue:* *Sue, new, chew, clue, few, chews, Drew, blue, blew, grew, true, flew, glue*

Phonics Skill Inflected Endings *-es* and Plural *-es:* *wishes, boxes, teaches, kisses*

Spelling Words: *new, grew, Drew, blue, true, glue*

Ty's New Baseball

REVIEW

by Dwight Anthony
illustrated by Deborah White

"I can't pitch," said Ty.
"My baseball is busted. We
can't play a ballgame with it."
"We can see if we can fix
it," said Betty, Jessy, and Lew.

"Can we glue it?" Betty
asked.

"No," said Ty. "We had
many happy games with this
ball. It's time to get a new
ball."

"Let's go inside," Lew said.
"Maybe my daddy can help
us get a new baseball."

"I do not have a clue," said Lew's daddy. He was cleaning dishes as he spoke.

"Use my lucky penny," said Ty. "We can make wishes on it."

"Wishes will not help,"
said Lew's daddy. "Try to
think of things you can do."

Ty, Lew, Jessy, and Betty sat on boxes in Lew's tent.

"Maybe we can do a few jobs," said Ty.

"Yes! We can get cash to get a new ball," said Jessy.

"We can paint mailboxes," Ty said.

"We can put on a funny show," Betty said. "I can do handstands."

"Let's make up a show," Lew said. "We can sing and play many games."

"Why not?" Ty asked. "We can make a funny show."

Lew, Betty, Ty, and Jessy gave a show.

Ty made ice cream pies.
Lew made funny handprint
animals. Betty painted faces
blue and green. Jessy had a
gum chewing contest.

"Now we have cash.
We can get a new baseball,"
said Ty. "We can play a
ballgame."

Phonics Skill Vowel Sounds of _y_ (long _i_ and long _e_): _Ty, my, Betty, Jessy, many, happy, daddy, lucky, penny, try, funny, why_

Phonics Skill Compound Words: _baseball, ballgame, inside, maybe, mailboxes, handstands, handprint_

Phonics Skill Vowel Pattern _ew, ue_: _Lew, glue, new, clue, Lew's, few, blue, chewing_

Phonics Skill Inflected _-es;_ Plural _-es:_ _dishes, wishes, boxes, mailboxes_

Spelling Words: _funny, many, my, why, new, blue, glue_